POST MOXIE

Post Moxie

Poems

Julia Story

Winner of the 2009 Kathryn A. Morton Prize in Poetry
Selected by Dan Chiasson

Sarabande Books
LOUISVILLE, KENTUCKY

Managing Editor
Sarabande Books, Inc.
2234 Dundee Road, Suite 200
Louisville, KY 40205

Library of Congress Cataloging-in-Publication Data

Story, Julia, 1974–
  Post moxie : poems / by Julia Story.—1st ed.
    p. cm.
  "Winner of the 2009 Kathryn A. Morton Prize in Poetry selected by Dan
  Chiasson."
  ISBN 978-1-932511-84-0 (pbk. : alk. paper)
  I. Chiasson, Dan. II. Title.
  PS3619.T6935P67 2010
  811'.6—dc22
                              2009035358

ISBN-13: 978-1-932511-84-0

Cover art: Louise Bourgeois, *Femme Maison,* 1947. Ink and pencil on paper.
9 15/16 inches x 7 1/8 inches (25.2 x 18 cm). Solomon R. Guggenheim Museum,
New York. 92.4008.

Cover and text design by Kirkby Gann Tittle.

Manufactured in Canada.
This book is printed on acid-free paper.

Sarabande Books is a nonprofit literary organization.

The Kentucky Arts Council, the state arts agency, supports
Sarabande Books with state tax dollars and federal funding
from the National Endowment for the Arts.

CONTENTS

FOREWORD

*B*AD BOOKS OF POEMS HAVE A LIFE OF THEIR OWN; so do great ones. Everything in between is dreary official business. The feeling of writing faultlessly is something every poet knows: some mistake it for brilliance. But the good-enough poems, the good-enough poets, are just prefects enforcing poetry's curfew, keeping poetry in line.

Julia Story's remarkable poems are, literally and in lots of other ways, out of line. A glimpse at the pages that follow will suggest the strange relationship these prose-blocks create to poetry's usual forms. You wouldn't call them "prose poems," implying the unbelievably drained tones and attitudes of that anemic genre. Prose poems don't thread the needle the way Story's poems do. Her narrow straits suggest the discipline of traditional forms. Her poems are about as wide, and often about as long, as sonnets.

The sonnet sequence is a nice analogy for Story's poems. The phrase "Story's poems" suggests what I mean: as in Petrarch or Shakespeare, George Meredith or Robert Lowell, the narrative current drives us downstream, but swirlingly, through endless eddies. These poems—arranged as they were written, and written (or so I would guess) as things happened—want to be read as simultaneously telling a story and keeping the story from being told.

When I called Julia Story to congratulate her, I compared her poems to slides projected onto a screen. She responded with a much finer perception: her friend called them tarot cards. They are tarot cards. It is interesting to think about why the latter analogy is so much better than the former. When you see a slideshow, what you see through the fog of your boredom is another person's life (the canonical emblem of twentieth-century boredom being precisely that: having to sit through slides of someone's vacation). But tarot cards establish, within oneself, a zone of mystery requiring tarot cards to explore. This is what all poems, in a way, do: hide the self, then propose their own terms for uncovering it. This is the game poets play with themselves, which in turn becomes the game they play with their readers.

But the tarot's inherited symbols—not the symbols one would have chosen, perhaps, but all the symbols we have on hand—suggest the really extreme, and extremely moving and beautiful, predicaments of these poems. Predicament one: we memorize and internalize what people tell us about ourselves: "Because I'm afraid of change, I wear the quilted pants emblazoned with pale peach skulls and crossbones." "I'm blonde and from Indiana so I look at the floor and smile." Examples like this abound: you are afraid of change; you are from Indiana. These ingrained interpretations— insults, in fact—are the gift a person gets from allowing herself to be known. Predicament two: poetry isn't really much better. Poetry's clumsy forensics are explored in an extraordinary poem near the beginning of this book. None of these poems have titles (Story calls them "stanzas," suggesting that they be read as a single poem), so I'll call it "For six years . . .":

> For six years the girls careen in his dream
> like little flashlights. My intelligence is
> measured by the number of sweat bees in
> the yard. In late fall I am not very smart.
> I am not very smart at the beginning
> of spring, when even the sidewalk has
> hormones. One little girl peeks out from

behind a factory wall far far away from a
backyard. She says This is how you make
it, and shows a handful of silver springs
and looks at him with blonde eyes.

"This is how you make it": every one of the poems in this book
should be emblazoned with that motto. The "little girl" in this
poem, displaced by the very fact of being in a poem (she is not just
"far" but, as in a fairy tale, "far far from a backyard") therefore
has to do the poem-like thing: revealing, as though by the opening
of her fist, a "handful of silver springs." (The history of poetry
could be subtitled "a handful of silver springs.") Story's writing
becomes deliberately, awkwardly "literary," since in poetry, "eyes"
always take an adjective. The wrongness of "blonde" implies how
threadbare this particular hand-me-down is.

Poems that think this carefully and provocatively about
themselves are scarce. But that's no reason to read a person's
poems. The misery and the total enchantment of being alive, of
being a complex person, mysterious even to oneself, and of feeling
like a cliché, of drawing from art and despising art, of thinking
simultaneously "fuck this" and "bring me more"—that's what got
put into this book, and that's what we get out of it.

Dan Chiasson

Post Moxie

THE ABOVE SONG

We look at a statue and feel uncomfortable. I am backward light, which isn't as cool as it sounds. Later, after I watch him eat his fake meat, he decides that he already knows everything there is to know about me based on a conversation we had about third grade. Because I'm afraid of change, I wear the quilted pants emblazoned with pale peach skulls and crossbones. From a distance they look like geometry. From up close, well, you can see what they look like up close.

He assures me that my head "doesn't look shaved" when he sees evidence of my late teen unhappiness. There are this many heads I want to break with this many bottles of Night Train, but I'm blonde and from Indiana so I look at the floor and smile.

Time is a series of pellets. The gerbil that sniffs them reacts by scratching his neck ferociously. It's my own fault I'm anywhere. When the rain in my mind begins, I don't run for cover. The pellets get wet and form a death paste. I stand there holding a cardboard box over my head. Or, more specifically, I have been standing there for weeks. Since after it rained.

You do *too* have a soul, I tell him absentmindedly while mending last year's swimsuit. I won't date anyone who can't buy his own ointment, I add. We aren't dating, we're adhering. I don't believe, I refer. "Oinkment," my neighbor from Portugal said sheepishly: the punch line to the first joke he learned in this crappy language.

But in the background, a cardinal. Tilting
his head and asking in a fog of bamboo,
bamboo in Indiana.

I said a marsh of words a swamp which
brings me back to the pants arranging
knick knacks on a sideboard while I
defended my rebound relationship with
a sex addict from Tucson do you know
that there are caverns in here tunnels
trap doors labyrinths I won't make a
porn with you won't discuss a thing by
candlelight

Do they not have those dogs anymore?
The neighbors with the toy dogs. The
new season meant they'd yip when I
walked by, exploding out their tiny door
like cannoned rats. The green mattress of
spring with its calling trees, its antidote
to heartbreak. But I refer rather than
believe. I have faith I'll keep thinking
the same things. Spring tries to sweep my
shadow into its maw. The good people of
earth want to help me but I don't believe
in this anymore.

Foie gras has been outlawed. So has
gravitas, faux grass, middle class.
Soon: the past

You're down the street trying to forget
about the Holy Spirit. That's your middle
ground for Christ's sake. That's what
died and entered you. The holy entrance.
Your entrails wound round and round
the world like red knitter's yarn, like a
ring of snakes before they turn into fire
and then turn back into dim gray waters
full of bored sharks.

"Bad to the Bone" plays overhead and embarrasses me. This is the worst first date ever, worse than the sad man with the trashed Firebird in his backyard. We walk down by the false lake and watch ducks sleep, their dull beaks tucked in, single tender eyes exposed. We wait over an hour for a table and then have to listen to the above song. Fortunately I can talk about work. He can't. If I line the books up perfectly, everyone will learn something. This is my favorite kind of business meeting: no one shows up.

For six years the girls careen in his dream like little flashlights. My intelligence is measured by the number of sweat bees in the yard. In late fall I am not very smart. I am not very smart at the beginning of spring, when even the sidewalk has hormones. One little girl peeks out from behind a factory wall far far away from a backyard. She says This is how you make it, and shows a handful of silver springs and looks at him with blonde eyes.

I write about a girl and then lose the
story I don't know where it went but
there is a Bible near me maybe it
went into the Bible and became a
different story a story about a girl
who lives

I bring her the new robin and she puts it on the shelf with the others. I have lost, I have lost, I have great loss is my song. The girl can wash up near me she can wear this mask and frighten away the dancers, the dream dancers, the dog dancers. The gray water will fill me instead. She doesn't want to hear this. She only wants to hear the delicate song of the worm.

It is hard to get the orchid to live
because it is easier to die. I want to
charge through the doorway of arms.
People can't stop me: illuminated under
lights, baking into different hardnesses.
Chatting and letting their eyes sink into
the corners where shabby sales reps wait,
growing polite and sleepy beneath the
dust-makers.

I bring her a whole tree ripped from the ground, its roots trailing mites and clingy damp clods. If I could get inside then everything would be ok: breadstick-shaped lights would quit falling all over me. When he finally took his stuff so he could let a shorter person take care of him, ants came in and bothered us. You poor thing, she tells me and rubs my forehead with bark and we carve a deep cavern inside us and rest for a while in the damp.

I look at myself and break. I burst into butterflies. But she knows me. She won't let me take this picture from my head again: the one where I point a knife at you and burst into pebbles, burst into poppies. I am on a blank landscape walking toward you but all you see are a pair of hands motionless on invisible hips.

The two cycles spin back on each other and the deer's chin hairs wobble as the rest of the hot heartland traffic whooshes. Many Jesus stickers bemoan nothing with their white crowns of thorns. A broken deer can break down into pavement, smaller and smaller until it becomes a bee. When a bee breaks, it takes its two parts to its own lake of sorrows, a hidden puddle with a shattered reflection: the destination of the world's tiniest heartbreaks.

Oh my boyfriend my boyfriend my boy-
friend. Ripper of a thousand wings.
Holder of a thousand hands.

I go to the field and I don't want him
to go but he goes anyway. He does fake
meditation in the woods while I do real
meditation with some dry grass and a
tree. She comes out of the woods to stand
among the golf balls and gnats. A black
dog makes a cutout on the horizon and a
boy in a towel cape runs from his invisible
enemy. I put my ear to the ground and
don't hear him think my name.

People I can't stand get drunk in sport sandals or make old-timey photographs of themselves in costume as if anyone cares about who they want to be. I coddle various babies for a living, wade fearless into the ocean if I can clutch my glasses. Curl up each night with the world's favorite books, lead the talentless on a covert crying mission across the Midwest. Coming to a mediocre city near you. Every fucking thing about me is designed to melt your heart.

The stairs go down to the subbasement's
dank bar. I wrap the scarf around my
neck three times and hurry past. Night
is coming down in a city I don't know.
The water-rat sky hands me my new life,
skinned, and the traffic fills with air.

ITS PLASTIC LIGHT

A new language for going undercover. The outfit for buying a wrench, the outfit for walking the dog, the outfit for staring at a wall. The tears are starting again, and the couples are staring at me, saying don't pretend it isn't summer. Don't pretend it's the saddest day of your life. A robin lands in the yard as I open my fifth beer. He eats some of the blue eggshell he carries, or stores it somewhere in his beak's cavern for a later purpose.

What is between us: two windows and a column of air. As I am my own mystic, I can collapse backward into dust babies. I'll bunny my way toward the fake horizon alone because I'm smarter than you. And faster.

The sun is a little motor that prepares us
for another day of faking the pretend sun
is actually the real sun is in the basement
I go down and down and down the stone
steps and dig up storms

A fig tree, the granite state, cicadas. Or locusts. I mean the limestone state. My neighbor drives his big stupid car over and asks do I want to go get breakfast. My words are vertebrae in a plastic bag. My silver urn is bending. My fig tree is a little girl's face tacked right through the eye. No, I say, I'm writing, then go back in to watch *Sixteen Candles*. I mean to say get under the covers but I'm already gone.

When I say you I mean hair-brained
muzzle-toothed   rat-bitten or however
you're appearing these days walking
hand in hand with yourself toward the
teacher of your dreams this is how you'll
get away from me while I drive air in
another state fill my ears with air fill my
tonsils with your voice

You stretch your arms out to crucify yourself but then change your mind. There is little to no weeping. I've made a pact with myself to not be crazy, but then there is that tree in the distance, clinging to itself and solid as a leg. Small dogs creep around the periphery of foliage. The nun in my head is of little to no use. The sounds of her lilies are like paper hands. When I wake up, it is to the white new air, no curtains, pedals outside spinning a cathedral.

Acne forms a delicate design, like pins in a map. It's important to know where stuff happened. My Nissan is broken. My dog won't stop barking. Everything would be ok if I could just rig up some paper lanterns and find a long extension cord and had the right kind of birthmark: a map of where to find you since the day I was born.

As delicate as an ass's bray are the little
lights which descend from the distant
city inside you can't pedal fast enough
to get there and when you finally do
catbirds have called it a day ears grow
dim you are barely a sound so you head
out again for the ring of trees

I'm in my membrane-colored sweater
and we watch the swirl of generic birds.
Tears enter your voice when you tell me
how long it's been since you fed them.
The sound all around us is not unlike
the crunching of dog food; the feeling is
November in a long year of not getting
laid. This is how I tell everything: ignore
the back throbbing. Lie down and turn
into trinkets.

The clunky parts of people collide like
water flowers. This is why we skip
dinner. Always in the ether something
waits for me to bring it in: its radish
voice hollowing like the backs of knees,
as vanished as a seed, as breathlike as
two people breathing.

I make the travel plans. When two ghosts cross each other, a sky is born. Two skies try to exist together, one in the background while the other takes the credit. Or one underneath the other, coiled like the furnace in a pretend hideout, waiting until it can be something else. The birds honking or in silent lines. This sound steadfast as a face.

I almost say bullshit but at the last
minute change it to malarkey. There
is room for me to stand on one foot.
I'm a latchkey kid, a circle denying the
evidence. Leaves descend all over the
borders, so many lines dividing one thing
or another to make a solid mesh through
which I can barely see.

I'm spending the winter here in the ash house on the edge of the crinkly sea. Darling I don't usually say darling but I want you to have everything behind my eyes. In the darkness your dark flashlight points out the room's troubles. I'll never have the really important ideas: I see only by the light of my skin.

Winter arrives in my head only. I take the longest path through the ice trees, the gray and hard lake, the bridge frozen and tooth-colored. Where I land makes no difference to me. The man in the distance waves and waves to get the birds off his hand. I wave back until the new man emerges from the blur: forklegged, with an upside-down anchor tattoo. We salute each other before hiking past, teacups quivering in our heads.

I had a dream one night that I was in
this like, war: the way things attach to
other things is like fighting: not breaking
apart but trying: the endings are like
stairways: the beginnings the beginnings
the beginnings are like pins: the boys
who won't love me take the hallway out
of town: nothing out of focus but the
doorknob

Do it without alchemy, he says. He has been asleep for several weeks. When he finally comes to I can't live with all the beauty. Something small, a small white taxi, scuttles in and out, a string connecting it to the larger and less important ground.

Soon I forget: a certain intake of breath, little things with the eyes, what a hand might do beyond official work. The night erects a platform so I can keep a safe distance from my sleep.

As trite as it sounds I'm busting out.
Several stamps deliver me to you: hi!
I'm in your dark bar playing Scrabble,
cowering over my highball so you won't
see. In your video I'm in the background
in purple mesh, blurring to amplified
wind. Or under your car repairing
something circuitous and dirty.

The cobbler is in Aruba they said but they'll have my shoes back to me by next week. I teleport to the astral plane or wherever. If I close my eyes the place I go is the basement as usual. The lamp gives its plastic light. I'm now at the stage where I write about crystals. When I smash it to pieces he hands me the crystal and its green light shows me the way through the dusty aisles.

Many have inserted candles here in order to worship the delicate flowers which grow from my eyelids. Corn in another county bends at the waist and the sky fills with specks of my inky radiance. Time breaks into manageable pieces around my great ending. I am crestfallen. Let me give you the apron of my love.

First take the tufts of hair the dog chewed off the fur pillows and bury them outside in the snow. The other things that need to be hidden will be listed soon. It helps to be on top of a mountain at dusk or to find the cabinets stocked with English supplies such as biscuits. The lawyers are still rich as are the dentists. Everything else has changed. I look frantically for something to puzzle me.

THE SKY IS A THING

I don't want to be like everyone else, yet I imagine myself attached to my own arm again. The parts of my head you don't see are grass-colored and glum. Dun was also a word I thought of. Other words that sound like dun. I look at things until they are vaguely identifiable piles, until the prettier rocks are within my reach.

Everything sounds like air as I walk from one end of the room to another. I prefer silence. It isn't the loneliness as much as the right angles everywhere that bother me. I'll think that I've finished my circle but there aren't any circles or enough crooners in the world to adequately express this.

He imagined what it would be like to live there, right down to the tent and the type of processed meat that could be cooked over a camp stove. I didn't really imagine it because I don't care about things like that, though I pretended in case there was a chance he might sleep with me. The hotel in the distance looked sad. I was field-colored and, in a certain light, field-shaped.

Dead Rockefellers, I'm not sure I'm cute enough. I don't think I want to live in the land of tables and receipts. John is dead and Sharon is alive is one thing I learned today. Ribbons of asphalt weave one of you into another, making you a road I ride further into this vault.

The truck bearing many logs falls over.
Cars stream to the sides of the road and
I wind backward into swirls of arms
and legs. The sky is a thing that must
be described as sweeping or radical.
I apologize for the cliffs which spring
out of every little thing I touch, for the
house which becomes smaller and more
abandoned.

Instead of going out and being expensive,
I want to look more carefully at hairs
and particles, lights in eyes, the dormant
humanity in a post-it. I can stare at a
glue stick for hours, at my fingernail
until night begins its dull blue waiting
and the wind blows over all of the lovers
with their ropes of lights, their ridiculous
sleeping.

I take my harp down to the water, but it isn't a harp, it's a person and we're falling in love. Birds land on us and I grip the air with my eyes. Hills are arms and the landscape is a bucket. His whole body is taped to me or taped to a picture of the world.

I give myself up piece by piece until the
day comes when there are no pieces I
bring myself a folded white dress as I
lie there sleeping and empty and glass
I wake up and put it on happy for this
dress which is a shard of light

I try to compare these things to the
spirals that occur in nature hold my ear
to air until it expands

What I hear is orange. A vase of fingers
is like a picture of a hand. A pitcher of
hands is the red haze under skin. The
red maze under all of us. I try to turn
this into something to rest on or the sky.
Pieces of people under all of what we say,
dingdonging into now.

By saying this you mock different colors.
The car ride to the fireworks was a
type of going under. Other types: fake
opiates, certain cows, one nose replaced
by another. The breasts rose and floated
above us when we vacuumed the sky.
I couldn't be tan enough. We weren't
here or in the sky but beneath the grass,
or an undergarment worn by a woman I
thought of only once.

Field walking, lap dance. I touch the tree
and explode out of here, mail myself back
and forth between a flower pot and eyes.
Dusk sinks in me. You walk the long hill
into your body and close the door.

Fucking mirrors. Reaching into a . . .
feeling. Pleiades a group of shadows on
the floor, flickering light to see me by.
Sadly the erotics of doubt.

Your dream inside my dream. Walked
the hill to the apartment where one
person mounts another. A stranger came
down the stairs to startle us. Before that
I screamed as you took out the trash in
your new ponytail. Then we remodeled
as the rain came down.

July a type of firebird, though I don't
know what a firebird is really. Something
that survived the fire. I've gone beyond
mere survival into a hallway that smells
like weed. Someone's abandoned shoes.
I'll never be serious enough to tell the
story, ambitious enough to stay awake.
This doesn't happen anywhere but still
there are clouds.

After I walked by the garden for the tenth time, the priest talked to me. He said, "Do you like the garden?" I told him that I hadn't seen it before, which was a lie. I don't want to create lessons for myself: it was a white afternoon with birds and traffic. I was in one of my outfits. The tomatoes were perfectly aligned and there were no weeds. He sat away from the garden and watched as I decided how to look at it.

I liked it better when things were blurred. Everyone understood that the world was a kind of story. Everything felt modern, but I was still behind the times in the wrong skirt. I thought the air underground would be cool or wormlike, but it was a different kind of red. When I breathed in fire I could only breathe out fire. No matter how much I looked at them, I couldn't become a tree. Breathing the leaves hurt too; they went into the nose wrong and didn't know how to keep from being real.

How to tell the story of what happened inside. You don't remember any of your dreams and your lover tells you not to use the word "love" in your complicated relationship analogy. Your ex-husband is even more ghostlike than the cartoon naked ladies in the basement. The day you'll understand this is marked on a calendar in your previous life.

It is good to be sad and say nothing. Clouds marry clouds over the ceiling. The girls in the town outside are young and angry with large sunglasses. Inside the town there are red eyes, red heels, red streets, red doors.

Too many bikinis here. Only teenagers
are this naked in Michigan. I prefer to
forgo the body altogether. If you can shut
me up long enough to take my picture,
I'll be that haze.

Float to Nantucket but never live there. Walk down the sidewalk while your head is in a tree. Or send your body out and keep the head carefully inside a TV. The body goes all over town wanting to buy stuff but the head put the credit card in the freezer. You have to break open the TV when you want something. You have to do this or else change your name.

There was no way to be fully alive. I did climb up onto the roof. I sat up there shaking while the bridge and a church were pointed out to me. The surface turned my legs and hands black. Already I was sliding down shingles watching the top of the neighbor's head as she took out the trash. Again and again I was somewhere else.

ACKNOWLEDGMENTS

Thank you to the following journals for publishing parts of *Post Moxie*:

Absent: "We look at a statue . . ."
            "Time is a series of pellets . . ."
            "I said a marsh of words a swamp . . ."
            "Do they not have those dogs . . ."
            "People I can't stand . . ."
            "You stretch your arms out . . ."
            "Acne forms a delicate design . . ."

Moonlit: "You're down the street . . ."
            "The two cycles spin back on each other . . ."
            "I make the travel plans . . ."

Octopus: " It is hard to get the orchid to live . . ."
            "As delicate as an ass' bray . . ."
            "I'm in my membrane-colored sweater . . ."
            "First take the tufts of hair . . ."
            "I take my harp down to the water . . ."

Indiana Review: "Winter arrives in my head only . . ."
                    "I don't want to be like everyone else . . ."

Free Verse: "Your dream inside my dream . . ."

Suss: "You do too have a soul . . ."
"For six year the girls careen . . ."
"Everything sounds like air . . ."

Thanks and love to my friend family and my biological family for their support. Special thanks to Heather Madden, Simeon Berry, Emilie Cushing, and Richard Lindley for helping me see the unseen.

Richard Lindley

JULIA STORY's childhood in Indiana was full of pets, grass, books, and Presbyterians. She earned graduate degrees in creative writing from The University of New Hampshire and Indiana University and has worked as a high school teacher, short order cook, secretary, store clerk, waitress, and professor. Her poetry was nominated for a Pushcart Prize and has appeared in *Octopus, Ploughshares, Sentence, The Iowa Review,* and other magazines. She lives in Somerville, Massachusetts.